Masks and Mask Makers

Iroquois Indian corn husk mask.
From the Museum of the American Indian.

Masks and
Mask Makers

Kari Hunt
and
Bernice Wells Carlson

New York   ABINGDON PRESS   Nashville

ISBN 0-687-23705-X
Library of Congress Catalog Card Number: 61-5097

To Our Children
    Karen, Christine, and Philip
And Our Husbands
    Douglas and Carl

Contents

Masks and Mask Makers

Why People Wear Masks

Why do you wear a mask on Halloween?

"To fool people."

"To make others guess who."

"To make others laugh."

Why do actors sometimes wear masks on the stage and on TV?

"To help them look like and act like a character in the play."

Why do firemen wear gas masks?

"To protect them when they enter a building filled with smoke."

These then are some of the reasons why people wear masks: (1) for disguise or to hide identity; (2) to transform a personality, make one person more like another person, animal, or spirit; (3) to protect a wearer against harm. Some ancient peoples also tried to preserve a personality by placing a mask upon the face of a dead person to help his soul travel to the after-life.

Although we wear masks at Halloween, or on the stage, or in a parade for fun, primitive people throughout the world wore them, and in some places still wear them, for very serious reasons. These reasons and the masks themselves are often interesting. This book pictures a large variety of masks and explains their uses.

A mask of the Basongo people, a Bantu tribe living between the Kasai and Lomami Rivers in the African Congo. From the University Museum of Philadelphia.

11

Masks for Disguise

No one knows exactly when or where or why a human being first covered his face with a mask; but we are sure that man has been doing it for a long, long time. Perhaps he first wore a mask to disguise himself.

A picture, found on the walls of a cave near Ariège, in southern France, shows men wearing animal skins and animal heads. This picture may have been painted 50,000 years ago, and the men may have been performing a ceremonial dance, or they may have been trying to frighten wild beasts away from their caves.

Some American Indians disguised themselves as animals in order to lure game close enough to shoot. An exhibit in the Smithsonian Institute, Washington, D. C., shows a Yosemite Indian wearing a deer skin, including the head. No doubt the hunter wanted to look like a deer so that a live deer would come close enough for him to kill it easily.

The Cherokee Indians of North Carolina also used animal masks to disguise themselves. But instead of wearing an animal head, the Indian hunter made a mask of hide and fur and tied it around his head. So disguised, he waited in the bushes until an animal came close enough for him to shoot.

In some primitive African tribes, even today, men and women wear masks for the fun of disguise. Men wear masks and mimic women. Women wear masks and mimic men. No one gets angry at anyone else because no one can identify the person who is poking fun at his neighbor.

In some parts of Africa and on some islands of the South Pacific Ocean, masks are worn by boys and girls in serious ceremonies which mark their entrance into adulthood. Parents know that their children are in the group, but no one knows which child is which.

Modern civilized people frequently wear masks as disguises, especially at parties and festivals. In the United States, boys and girls wear masks on Halloween when they go from house to house, saying, "Trick or treat?" Little children fail to recognize Santa Claus at a church or club party be-

Helmet secret-society mask of the Mendi people of Sierra Leone, West Africa. From the University Museum of Philadelphia.

cause he wears a mask. Both good men and bad men on TV wear masks which cover part of their faces and conceal their identity.

13

Masks for Transformation

At one time or another, primitive men in all parts of the earth have wondered about the world around them and asked, "Why does the sun shine?" "What makes the wind blow?" "Why is the bear stronger than I am?" "Why can the deer run faster than I?"

Centuries ago, early men decided that there must be spirits in the air, in animals, and in birds which had powers men did not have, but for which they longed. They thought, "If we imitate the animals, maybe we can have some of their spirits. If we capture a spirit that we cannot see, perhaps we can become part of that spirit."

So men made masks which were more than disguises, masks which they hoped would transform them, make them more like the creatures and spirits they wished to be: strong as a bear, fleet as a deer, wise as an owl. They gave names to the spirits which they thought controlled the world and made masks which they hoped would bring these spirits to them. They hoped the spirits would help them cure the sick, control the weather, insure good crops, and be victorious over their enemies. Men also believed that there were evil spirits in the world and made masks which would give them power over evil.

As time went by, they developed dances, ceremonies, and other rituals which they thought the spirits wanted them to perform. Gradually, these ceremonies became so complicated that in most tribes only certain carefully selected men learned them and were allowed to wear spirit masks. Every tribe had many kinds of masks, but the masks for any one ceremony were always the same. The mask of the God of Rain, for example, could always be recognized by all tribesmen.

Spirit masks have been discovered in all parts of the world, from frozen Alaska and Cape Horn to the broiling Congo. They have been made since the time of the Stone Age and are still made today. They are made of every kind of material: wood, animal skin and fur, shells, metals, stone, corn husks, bark cloth—anything available. Some masks are very

Wooden mask of the Eskimos of Alaska. In the Brooklyn Museum Collection.

simple. Some are elaborate and are skillfully carved of wood or stone or delicately hammered of metal and decorated with jewels, shells, bright stones, or feathers. Some resemble birds, animals, or humans. Others are fantastic creations, like nothing on earth. All are very important to the people who believe in the magic of masks.

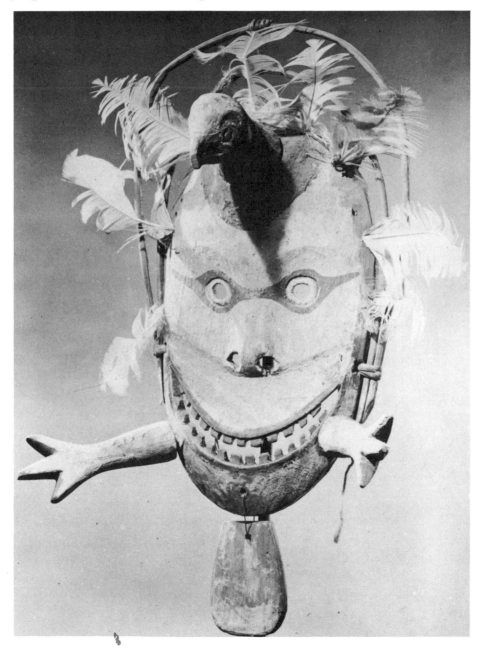

Masks for the Dead

The belief in an afterlife was widespread among ancient people in many parts of the world. They knew that the afterlife would be different from this life; yet they believed that man's needs would remain very much the same. Weapons, clothing, tools, even food and drink, were buried with the body of a beloved person, especially with the body of a chief or king. Finally a death mask was placed upon his face to preserve his personality and to help his soul on its travels.

Masks of this kind were used around the world. They may be seen today on Egyptian mummies in museums. They have also been found in Ecuador, Mexico, Phoenicia, Cambodia, Siam, Indo-China, Mesopotamia, Britain, central Europe, and other places.

In many parts of the world, especially in Africa and on islands of the South Pacific Ocean, people still believe that the spirits of their dead ancestors live among them. Elaborate masks are used in funeral ceremonies to persuade the spirit of the dead man to help his tribe. Other masks are used to call up the spirits of ancestors who have been dead for a long time. In New Ireland, an island in the South Pacific Ocean, natives hold rites each year to which, they believe, the spirits of all their dead ancestors return in masked form.

Certain primitive tribes seek to banish the spirits of the dead in rituals conducted by masked tribesmen. In some African tribes, funeral rites tell the spirit of the deceased how to find his afterlife and beg him not to return.

In New Guinea, after an elaborate funeral, all the masks and other paraphernalia which dancers have used, are placed on a raft and floated down the river to the sea. There, it is hoped, the raft will sink and the spirit of the dead person will become a crocodile, shark, or snake.

Funeral mask of New Ireland, in the South Pacific. In the Brooklyn Museum Collection.

Dramatic and Carnival Masks

As some people came to know more about the world around them, they stopped believing in the magic of masks. However, they sometimes continued the rituals and ceremonies as entertainment. People who took part in the revised ceremonies were chosen because they could sing, dance, and act, and not because they were religious leaders. In some cases, the rituals developed into plays, and in other cases into masked carnivals.

Some of the singers, dancers, and actors added pantomimed stories to the rituals, with a chorus explaining the plot in song. Later actors were given speaking parts; and eventually the play, as we know it, developed. In ancient dramas, actors wore masks to help them become the characters, not the spirits, they wanted to be. Masks are sometimes worn on the stage today for the same reason.

Some of the actors long ago put on masks and made merry as they acted out the ancient ceremonies in the market places or in the streets. Everyone had fun and gradually forgot that the masked celebrations once had religious meaning.

Halloween, as we know it, is certainly not a religious event. Yet, it developed from the belief that on the night before All hallows, or All Saints' Day, witches, ghosts, and imps, now represented by masked merry-makers, could do any amount of mischief until quieted at dawn by the spirits of the saints.

On festival days in Mexico, especially on Corpus Christi Day in June, people wear masks to frighten evil spirits away from homes and villages. No one believes in the magic of these masks, but people wear them for fun, as we wear Halloween masks.

Mardi Gras which is celebrated in France and in New Orleans, in this country, with big parades of masked merry-makers and with masked balls, is a festival of Shrove Tuesday, the last day when people can have a gay time before fasting and meditating during Lent. Other church days are celebrated with similar festivals in Europe and South America.

In China, India, and Java, there are processions and festivals in which

18

masked figures play an important role. These celebrations are also survivals of ancient religious ceremonies.

A festival mask of Java. Courtesy of the American Museum of Natural History.

19

Masks for Protection

Although most tribes of primitive people found masks too bulky to wear in actual battle, a few tribes wore them for protection. Warriors of the Tlingit Indians of the North West Coast of North America wore wooden helmets, with visors and yokes, which protected the wearer in battle. The *t'ao-t'ieh* mask of China may have originally served this purpose; and the war mask of ancient Japan not only protected the wearer but frightened the viewer as well.

The helmet of the medieval knight was a protective mask, although it is not classified as a mask in a museum. There are many stories about unknown knights, who stepped forward to win battles. Such a knight was disguised, and perhaps he was even transformed into a braver man than he would have been unmasked. Most certainly he was protected by the covering on his face.

Some Indian tribes of North America found protection in a different way. Warriors wore masks to conceal their emotions. An enemy could not tell if a masked man was afraid or hurt.

Often ancient masks protected their wearers in a less physical way. Some were supposed to scare an opponent, either human or spirit. In eighth-century Japan, twenty devil dancers with especially powerful masks, protected the royal palace from demons.

Today masks form useful functions every day. Welders wear shields to protect their faces from flying sparks. Baseball catchers and hockey players who guard the goals wear masks to protect their faces from foul balls and flying pucks. Deep sea divers wear masks to keep water from entering their eyes and sometimes their noses. Firemen and soldiers wear gas masks when they enter a building filled with smoke or harmful fumes. Doctors and nurses wear masks in an operating room to protect a patient from germs. Space flyers wear masks to assure a supply of oxygen.

Ancient Japanese suit of armor. Courtesy of the Metropolitan Museum of Art. Gift of Edith McCagg, in memory of Louis B. McCagg, 1929.

Eskimo and American Indian Masks

Before European men dreamed of a new world, Eskimos and Indians of both North and South America wore masks as part of their religious ceremonies. These masks were as different as the civilizations of the men who wore them.

The simplest and crudest masks were made and worn by some Eskimos of Alaska and by the Ona Indians who lived near Cape Horn in South America. These primitive men took a piece of rawhide, shaped it like a face, cut out eyes and mouth, decorated it with one bright spot of paint, and tied it on. The spot allowed the spirit to enter the mask.

The most elaborate and beautiful masks in America were made by the highly civilized Inca Indians of Peru and by the Maya and Aztec Indians of Mexico. Masks carved of stone, turquoise, and green onyx, or fashioned of gold, copper, clay, and silver were placed on the faces of the dead to help them on their way to the afterlife. Other elaborate masks were worn by priests in the temple ceremonies.

Some of the Indian tribes of the Northeast, Southwest, and Eastern United States and Canada made masks intricately carved of wood, painted in bright colors and often decorated with feathers, fur, or hair.

The plains Indians of North America did not make masks but often wore the heads and skins of animals in ceremonial dances.

God mask of the Inca Indians, from Tiahunaca, Peru. Courtesy of the American Museum of Natural History.

Eskimo Masks of Alaska

The primitive Eskimos of Alaska believe that the world is filled with many spirits or souls: spirits of the elements, such as spirits of the wind, the sun, and the moon; spirits of places; and spirits of things, especially things that people need, such as food. Each person has a number of souls: one soul returns to earth again and again; other souls are for different parts of the body, a soul for the head, a soul for each arm, etc. Animals, too, have souls. The success of a hunt depends upon the animal's willingness to be killed, serve as food for man, become a spirit soul, and return to earth in a new life to again be hunted by men.

The Eskimo feels that he must know how to treat these souls and magic spirits that control the earth. There are many taboos he must observe, words he cannot say and things he cannot do without offending a spirit.

Among the Eskimos are a few men and women who are thought to have the power to see these spirits in dreams or trances. These people become shamans, or medicine men, and have great authority. After a shaman has seen a spirit, he copies its image in mask form, often carving it out of wood. As a rule, the mask more or less resembles a man, a beast, or a bird; but one feature is usually distorted—one eye is out of place or the mouth and nose are not in line. The mask becomes a link between the shaman and the spirit. When the shaman wears the mask, he becomes a spirit and can control what the spirit does.

Almost every family has a shaman. Every village has several.

The shaman has many duties. He must forecast the weather, predict where hunters can find game, and tell how to defeat an enemy if the tribe is confronted with one. He must protect the tribe from all evil spirits.

The most important job of a shaman is to cure a sick person. Sickness, in the Eskimo's mind, is caused by someone's breaking a taboo and so offending a spirit. By performing certain ceremonies, for which a mask is worn, the shaman may persuade the spirit to let the sick person recover.

Mask of Alaskan Eskimos, Hooper Bay. From the University Museum, Philadelphia.

24

The Eskimos hold many festivals to give thanks for successful hunts and to help the tribe win favor with various spirits. At a festival, masked shamans dance around a dimly lighted fire with tufts of fur and feathers, which extend from their masks, swaying back and forth making weird shadows on the walls. Faster and faster they dance and stamp, howling, beating tambourines, and calling to the spirits in a secret language. The watchers feel certain that the spirits will bless the tribe.

Northwest Indian Masks

The Indians who lived in Northwestern America, from southern Alaska to northern California, believed that all things, and especially animals, had special spirits. They carved fantastic masks of wood to help identify themselves with these spirits. Many of the masks had moveable parts which could be operated by cords.

These Indians told many legends about the early stages of the world. In those days, they said, men roamed the woods disguised as birds or animals. If they wanted to assume human form, they pushed up their beaks or muzzles, as we might lift a mask.

As these legends were told, they were often acted out. A legend might begin, "There stood a raven, and suddenly the raven became a man." When this was acted out, a dancer, wearing a raven mask, entered the room. At the right moment, he pulled a cord, revealing the face of a man.

These Indians believed that the spirits were most likely to visit people during cold weather. Therefore, ceremonial dances were performed on winter evenings with members of the tribe sitting around a glowing fire.

Tribesmen believed that inspiration for these ceremonies came directly from guardian spirits. A man, consulting his guiding spirit, might suddenly see it appear in the shape of an owl. The owl would tell him exactly how to make his mask and how to perform a dance. The Indian would announce that he had had a vision and would select a few men to help him in the ceremonial dance.

Masks were always made in secret and hidden until used. Performers practiced in secret. They created stage effects which added to the awesomeness of the performance. Trap doors and tunnels allowed dancers to appear and disappear suddenly. Hollow kelp-stem speaking tubes permitted voices to come from anywhere: the air, the fire, or beneath the spectators.

On the night of the ceremony, the masked dancers hid until the appointed time. Then into the circle of watchers they rushed, screaming,

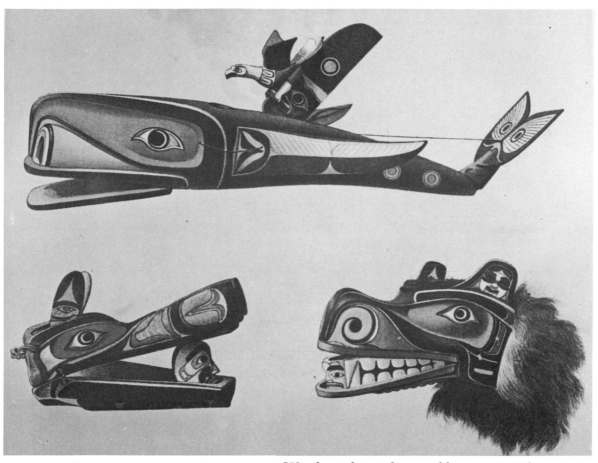

Wood masks with movable parts, made by the Kwakiutl Indians of Vancouver Island, British Columbia. Courtesy of the American Museum of Natural History.

dancing wildly, and frightening even the most stalwart members of the tribe.

In some tribes, after the dance was over, the masks were carefully preserved and handed down from father to son. In other tribes, masks for certain ceremonies were used once and then destroyed. Other masks were kept for a specific period of time, in some cases for four years, and then destroyed.

Iroquois Masks

The Iroquois Indians, which include many tribes in Eastern United States and Canada, are noted for two kinds of masks: twisted face masks made of basswood, and husk face masks.

A legend explains the origin of the twisted face mask. When the Maker had finished the earth, he banished all evil spirits and started westward. On the way, he met the head of the False Faces. The two argued about who should control the earth and agreed to have a contest to see who could best command a mountain.

The False Face shook his turtle rattle and commanded the mountain to move. It did so. Pleased with his success, the False Face turned his face away from the Maker and the mountain. The Maker then commanded the mountain to stand next to the False Face. The mountain obeyed quickly. When the False Face turned his head, he bumped it on the mountain, broke his nose, and twisted his mouth.

The Maker then gave the False Face the tasks of driving disease from the earth and aiding travelers and hunters. The False Face accepted the jobs and added an agreement. If men would make portraits of him from basswood, call him grandfather, and offer him tobacco and mush, they, too, could cure the sick and aid hunters and travelers by blowing hot ashes on them.

According to another legend, the False Face taught the Indians how to carve the masks from a standing tree, so that the spirit of the tree could go directly into the mask. The mask was painted red if carved in the morning, and black if carved later in the day. Each mask had twisted features and shovel-like lips which permitted the wearer to blow ashes on the sick.

The Husk Face masks represented spirit farmers that the Iroquois thought lived on the other side of the earth. These spirit farmers would visit the Iroquois in their longhouses during a two-night midwinter festival. Masked dancers would arrive with great din, stop the dancing, and capture a chief for an interpreter.

Iroquois False Face Society masks. Courtesy of the American Museum of Natural History.

After talking to the Husk Faces, the chief would announce that the visitors were messengers of three sisters, corn, beans, and squash, and that the strangers had the power of prophecy. If asked to dance with the merry-makers, the Husk Faces were said to insure the fertility of the crops. Of course, everyone urged the Husk Faces to join in the dancing.

Indian Masks of the Southwest

Rain is the one thing which Indians of the dry sections of southwestern United States need more than anything else. Without rain, their crops of corn dry up, there is no grass for sheep to nibble, and they themselves may die of thirst. What brings the rain? Spirits, the Indians say. Spirits rule the sky, earth, sun, rain, clouds, wind, and all the elements. And so the Indians dance for the spirits to bring the rain.

Two of the Pueblo Indian tribes, the Hopi and Zuni, believe that once upon a time many little gods or spirits, called *kachinas*, dwelt among men and brought them corn and water. When the *kachinas* left the villages to live forever in the bottom of a desert lake, they left masks behind to help them return to man. The Indians believe that when they put on masks and dance, they themselves become gods or *kachinas*.

All men in these tribes own masks which are made in secret under the direction of *kachina* priests who, according to legend, are chiefs of the spirit world. These priests tell the tribesmen exactly how to make the masks and other parts of the ceremonial costumes and how to perform the ritual dances. Some authorities say that these ritual ceremonies are so important to the Pueblo Indians that the men spend half their time in religious activities.

The most important dance is the Shalako, the rain dance. If rain fails to fall when expected, the Indians feel that something was wrong with the ritual dance or ceremonial dress. Maybe a wrong color was used on a mask. Maybe a feather was out of place or a dancer out of step.

There are more than 100 traditional Pueblo masks. Some are repainted or replaced after each ceremony; but the masks of the priests remain the same. The honor of becoming a priest is inherited.

Masks worn by the Apache and Navaho Indians of the Southwest resemble those of the Pueblos' in color and shape. In these two tribes, however, only medicine men make and wear masks. They are used until they are worn out or until their magic disappears.

30

Indian Masks of South America

The primitive Takun Indians who live in the forests of Brazil, Peru, and Colombia along the Amazon River hold festivals in which masked dancers ward off evil spirits and celebrate important events.

One elaborate festival is held when a girl becomes a woman, at the age of twelve or thirteen. For three months before the festival, the girl is hidden in an elevated hut, away from the eyes of men and from the grasp of evil demons. Then, when the moon is right, Indians come in canoes from miles around, bringing their own food, their own hammocks in which to sleep, and their own garments and masks for the ceremonial dances of the three-day festival.

During the ceremonies, some of the dancers masquerade as monkeys, wearing long bark-cloth garments and masks with popping eyes and pointed snouts. Other dancers wear long white bark-cloth sacks, topped by weird forest-demon masks. One dancer wears the mask of the jaguar, king of the Amazon forest. Guests and relatives of the maiden dance, sing, eat, and drink for two days and nights.

At dawn of the third day, the maiden joins them for initiation ceremonies. Her body has been painted black and bright red with urucú dye. She wears a wide beaded belt, many strings of beads and bracelets, and a high crown of macaw feathers which covers her eyes. (If she can see, evil spirits may harm her.) Ritual dancing continues all day to protect the maiden from evil. As the sun sets and the moon rises, a witch doctor appears, hands the young woman a firebrand, and charges her to throw it against her worst enemy. She slings it against a tree, believing she is casting out lurking forest-demons.

Then comes a strange ceremony. As the maiden kneels on a mat, relatives pull out her hair, a few strands at a time, until she is bald. She then puts on the feathered crown, this time with eyes uncovered, and dances until dawn.

Early in the morning, the guests sweep the house of the host and depart, leaving behind them the costumes and masks they have worn. The costumes will be used as sleeping bags and the masks will be burned in a few months, at another ceremony. The maiden is now ready to marry, although she will probably wait until her hair has grown.

Clown costume of bark cloth by South American Indians of the Amazon region. Courtesy, American Museum of Natural History.

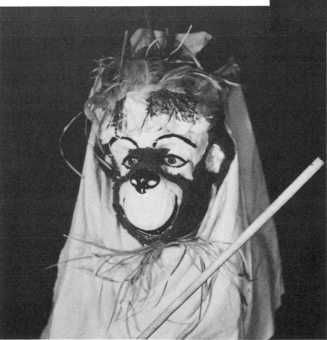

Monkey mask of the South American Indians. From the Hunt Collection. Photograph by Douglas Hunt.

Masks of Africa and the South Pacific

Many natives of Africa and some of the South Pacific Islands, especially those islands known as Melanesia, hold similar beliefs. Most of these people believe in supernatural spirits, and they think that masks help men speak with these spirits. In fact, they believe that when a man puts on a mask, he becomes a spirit himself with supernatural power.

These primitive people have a great respect for, and fear of, the dead. They wish to do everything possible to please the dead souls, and therefore hold many ceremonies in their honor. Masks play an important part in these rituals.

Masks worn in these ceremonies in Africa are not images of people who are dead, but they often look something like one individual or another. Sometimes a mask bears a scar, or a particular hair style, or some other mark which identifies it with a specific soul. The masks worn by natives of the South Pacific for similar rituals are unlike the African masks in that they are never identified with individuals.

Many of these people also believe in protective animal spirits, protective bird spirits, and protective fish spirits. Therefore, a mask may assume the general shape of an animal, bird, or fish. Or it may take the shape of a spirit seen in a dream, and be like nothing else on earth.

Spirit mask of Baluba, Kabanda, Africa. Courtesy of the American Museum of Natural History.

African Witch Doctor Masks

One of the beliefs common to most primitive people is the belief that sickness is caused by offended spirits. In Africa, the men who are supposed to persuade these spirits to cure a patient are called witch doctors.

Every witch doctor has certain "sacred" paraphernalia: horns, sticks, etc., which he inherited from his father who was also a witch doctor. He also has powders and drugs, made by secret formulas. And he is almost certain to have a mask. The mask itself is not regarded as magic; but when a witch doctor puts it on, he is thought to become the spirit of an ancestor who has power to cure or not cure a patient.

In Kenya, a traveler saw parents bring a sick child to a witch doctor. He treated the parents, not the child, because the tribe believed that the parents must have offended a spirit.

The parents knelt beside a banana leaf on which there lay a thick brown mixture which included a "must" of African medicine, the undigested contents of a goat's stomach taken while the goat was still alive. The witch doctor, wearing a mask, placed some of the entrails of the goat on the parents' shoulders. He added powders to the brown mixture, chanting as he worked, and stirred the brew. Then he dipped the tips of a ram's horns into the mixture and thrust the tips of the horns into the parents' mouths. They promptly spit out the stuff, hoping that the child was then cured.

Another role of the witch doctor in this tribe is to "bless" young men who want to raid their neighbors' cattle. Before starting out, the raiders approach the witch doctor who dons his mask and consults the spirits. If they approve of the raid, he brings out a pair of waterbuck horns, decorated with feathers, rags, broken egg shells, and other things. Next he makes a paste of medicine which he rubs on the arms and legs of the raiders to protect them from spears and arrows. Then, while the witch doctor chants, each raider touches the magic horns. After this, the raid cannot fail, unless someone offends a spirit before they reach the cattle.

36

*Hood mask, with cowery shells and beads,
Bakuba tribe of the Congo. From the Segy
Gallery for African Art.*

Dogon Masks for the Dead

The natives of Africa have mixed emotions about the dead. They would like to love them; but they fear them because they believe that the dead spirits control their lives. One way to protect a village from the spirits of the dead is to chase them away.

After a death, the Dogon tribe of the French Sudan conducts very elaborate morning services which last six days and are designed to chase away the soul of the dead person. On the first day, natives march in procession to caves near the village where masked dancers form a circle and perform a ritualistic ceremony. Every man in the village has a special crossbow he uses on certain occasions. At the end of the dance, dancers pick up the dead man's crossbow and carry it in state to a specified spot.

At sunrise of the second day, dancers go to the dead man's house where they perform dances to force the dead man's soul to leave the grounds and go outside the village.

By the third day, the handle of the dead man's hoe and the cups from which he drank have been placed in a field. The dancers perform another ritual in this field, at the close of which they pick up the dead man's hoe handle and cups, carry them to some bushes, and break them. Never again will the dead man, or his ghost, till the soil, or drink.

Finally on the sixth day, dancers perform a "wiping of the feet" ceremony, the last public act to banish the ghost.

Helmet type masks, partly open at the back, are worn for these ceremonies. They are held in place by cords or wooden handles.

The dancers also wear red fiber ruffs around their necks and skirts dyed in brilliant colors, which make them look more like creatures of a spirit world than like men. This, the natives think, is as it should be. When a man puts on this mask and this costume, he becomes part of a spirit which will drive the ghost away.

Mask of the dead from the Dogon Tribe in the African Sudan. Photograph from the Segy Gallery for African Art. Used by permission.

Masks of the South Pacific

Among the masks used on the South Pacific Islands, known as Oceania, are the peace masks worn in New Ireland on May 1. On this day, all men, many of whom have been deadly enemies, don red shirts, fern skirts, and masks which they have made during the year. They paddle to a certain spot where they spend the day feasting and dancing.

At the close of the day, something always happens. One warrior may laugh at another's mask, or in some way offend him. A fight starts, everyone takes sides, and men become deadly enemies for another year. Then, when May 1 comes again, they all put on new masks and celebrate another peace day.

Most of the masks used on these islands are worn for serious ceremonies, however. Masks are used in rites honoring ancestors, preparing boys for manhood, burying the dead, and blessing hunting or fishing expeditions.

All of these island dwellers believe that mythical and ancestoral spirits rule their lives, and that evil spirits lurk everywhere. Many masked dances are held in honor of the spirits. A mask is thought to bring forth a spirit and make it visible. Therefore, each mask is made with great care. When a native puts on a mask and picks up a ceremonial stick, he believes that an ancestor is actually guiding his actions as he dances.

Some of these masks are beautifully carved of wood and are exquisite in their simplicity. Others are decorated with shells or painted with multicolored symbolic designs.

The natives of New Guinea make huge masks, built on wicker frames, that tower from nine to thirteen feet into the air. Above these frames, float feathers and other decorations, making the entire mask at least twenty feet high. Sometimes as many as one hundred of these masks are used in one ceremony.

Masked dancer representing clan ancestor in masked pageant of New Guinea. Courtesy of the American Museum of Natural History.

Masks of the Far East

Most of the masks of the Far East are worn by pantomime dancers in ceremonies which are both religious and theatrical. All of the dances started as religious rites, and many are still performed by priests and lamas. Others are no longer thought of as religious and are done only because they are beautiful and people enjoy watching them.

All of the dances follow a general pattern, which we roughly call Oriental or stylized dancing. Every movement has a meaning which is understood by the audience. Every dance has its own pattern. Every mask, robe, and piece of property follows a special design.

In Ceylon, there are nineteen standard masks which priests wear in performing the rites to cure diseases by driving out devils. To cure a fever, for example, the priest wears a red mask. He dances in front of his patient until the demon is lured from the patient and into his own body. He falls as if dead and is carried out of the village where he remains until he is sure that the devil of the disease is gone.

In China, Buddhist and Taoist priests produce entertaining and educational plays, designed to encourage men to follow Buddhist teachings. In some scenes, demons and devils, wearing fantastic masks, pester and torture men who have forsaken the life of prayer and meditation. Other scenes depict the peace of the righteous man.

Nineteenth-century, painted wood ceremonial mask of Ceylon. In the Brooklyn Museum Collection.

42

Rangda Masks of Bali

Rangda, queen of the witches, who once was thought to control all the forces of evil in the East Indies, has been declared officially dead by the Mohammedans. But in remote villages, especially on the island of Bali, natives still fear her evil spirit which spreads plague, steals and devours babies, and causes all manner of disaster.

According to legend, Rangda was the wife of a king and the mother of King Erlangga who united Java and Bali into one kingdom during the eleventh century. When her husband died, she fled into the forests to escape dying on the funeral pyre, the fate of all widows of her day. (The word *Rangda* means *widow*.) In the forest, she became a witch and summoned all the evil spirits to do her bidding.

When a village feels that some misfortune is about to come, natives hold a Rangda dance in the hope of appeasing her and persuading her to spare them. A dancer puts on a Rangda mask, a horrible creation made of wood, painted white, with bulging eyes, animal-like teeth, fangs reaching both up and down, monkey-like ears, and a long, lolling leather tongue, painted gold. Light stringy hair, five feet long, tops this horrible mask. People feel that when a woman puts on this mask and dances the Rangda dance, she actually becomes Rangda. Rangda and dancers who perform with her, dance in a trance, as do many dancers in the East Indies.

The rite begins with maidens dancing before a sacred flame of sweet-smelling leaves. Into the scene rushes Rangda, screaming and uttering unearthly sounds as she prances around wildly. Her long white hair nearly reaches the ground and her golden tongue flaps upon her chest.

Soldiers enter the scene and dance frantically around Rangda, finally stabbing themselves with small daggers. Although they draw blood, they are not hurt because they are in a trance. At last Rangda leaves the scene and everyone hopes that she has decided not to call the evil spirits down upon the village.

Now and then a visitor is allowed to buy a Rangda mask which priests

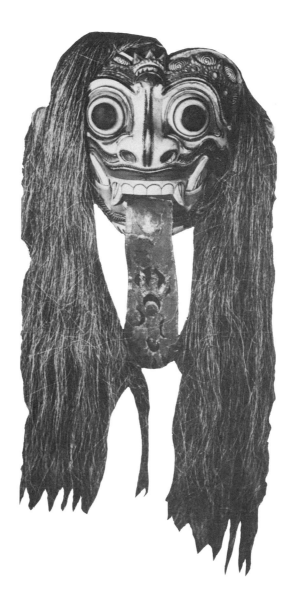

Rangda Mask of Bali. From the Hunt collection. Photograph by Douglas Hunt.

say has lost its power. However, the buyer must promise to take the mask away from the island and never bring it back.

45

Masks of Tibet

In Tibet, tucked away in the Himalayan Mountains, are the best examples of masks which are used today in dramas based on religious rites. As far back as the seventh century, Tibetan people held ceremonies with masked dancers. The dancers were thought to have the power to ward off evil spirits and influence deities who could bring blessings to the people. With the coming of Buddhism, these rites were developed into elaborate mystery plays presented by masked monks and lamas to show what happens to men who fail to follow the teachings of Buddha.

These plays are produced exactly as they have been produced for centuries. They are given in a temple yard with no theater, no stage, and no scenery. There is no melodic music; but the pantomimes are accompanied by outcries of tortured souls, tramping feet, blaring trumpets, and clanging bells.

The dramas and plays are presented during the many festivals held throughout the year. The greatest of these is the New Year, which comes early in February and marks the anniversary of the coming of Buddhism to Tibet as well as the end of the old year. Vast crowds of pilgrims, people from all walks of life, wind their way up the mountainside to the temple to watch a performance which lasts half a day. There may be as many as 5,000 spectators huddled together in one temple yard.

The story for New Year centers around Yama, king and judge of the inferno. Assisted by eighteen judges and many demons, he decides into which hell each wayward soul shall go for torment. This is complicated because, according to Buddhists, there are eight major hot hells situated under the earth. These are subdivided into one hundred twenty-eight smaller hot hells. In addition, there are eight cold hells, eight dark hells, and eighty-four thousand small hells on the edge of the universe. At the end of the play, the lamas burn a sheet of paper on which is written all the evil happenings from which the natives wish to be protected during the coming year.

Each character in a Tibetan drama wears a stylized mask which is

46

always the same for that character. They are huge, helmet-type masks, made of papier mâché and brightly painted, so that the large audiences can easily see them.

Papier mâché mystery play masks of Tibet, a guardian king and an aerial demon. Courtesy of The Newark Museum, Newark, New Jersey.

No Masks of Japan

Masks are worn in Japan for many kinds of festivals; but their most unique use is in the Nō dramas, musical plays which have remained unchanged since the sixteenth century. These plays were probably started as a combination of pantomime dances performed at Shinto festivals and poetic songs written by Buddhist monks. They were written down by a man named Kiyotsugu. His son Motokiyo added songs and improved the music. There are more than 200 of these plays; but they are so beautifully poetic, so hard to understand, and so artistically presented that they appeal only to the most educated of the Japanese.

These plays are not religious, but tradition says that they were invented for a goddess. Amaterasu, the sun goddess, was once offended and went into a cave to pout. With her she took all the sunshine of the world. Of course, no one liked living in the darkness that remained. So the other gods got together on the River of Heaven (The Milky Way) to plan what should be done. They tried in various ways to lure the sun goddess from the cave; but all in vain. At last they aroused her curiosity by inventing a new kind of dance, performed on an inverted tub which echoed as they stamped with bare feet. She heard this loud, yet deadened, sound and left her cave to see what was making it. At once the world was light again.

Dancing on a specially constructed elevated stage which echoes with a resounding noise when actors stamp with slippered feet is still an important part of the Nō drama.

Everything about the Nō drama is always exactly the same. Only men act, so actors portraying women wear masks that represent the standard type of beauty, a narrow white face with eyebrows painted high on the forehead. Other masks represent ghosts, demons, old people, heroes, men, gods, and goddesses. There are at least 125 varieties of Nō masks.

The stage for a Nō drama is bare, except for three living pine trees and one painted pine tree, always placed in the same positions. The chorus

48

Lacquered wood masks for Nō drama, old man and woman. Courtesy of The Newark Museum, Newark, New Jersey.

sits in a certain spot and chants the plot of the play in poetry, accompanied by musicians who also have appointed positions. Every gesture of every actor is always the same and has a special meaning for the educated audience.

A Nō play is about one hour long. However, six plays are usually given in one day, with short funny dances in between performances.

Masks in Civilized Europe

No one knows when the people of Europe started to make masks; but we have every reason to believe that peasants were wearing false faces for special events before the days of Greek and Roman glory.

The early Greeks wore masks in certain religious ceremonies. These developed into dramas for which false faces were always worn. The Romans, who copied the Greeks, also wore masks for plays. They wore them, too, in parades and at feasts.

During the Middle Ages, masks were worn by both professional and amateur actors who performed in court yards, village squares, and castles. They were also worn at many festivals which had remote connections with religious holidays; and feast days became days of masked revelry. Large parades were held in most countries with masked villagers prancing up and down the streets and playing tricks. Masked balls, to which men and women wore tiny masks which covered only the eyes and upper part of the nose, became very popular. So disguised, dancers felt a little bolder than they would have felt unmasked.

Little by little, masks became more and more associated with fun. In eighteenth century England, from Twelfth Night (twelve days after Christmas) until Lent, men and women put on masks at the slightest excuse and did mischief they might not otherwise have done.

Today in Europe, most large cities and many villages hold festivals and parades where masks play an important role in the merry-making.

European half-mask. From the Hunt collection. Photograph by Douglas Hunt.

Greek Masks

The early Greeks wore animal masks (pigs, horses, and cats) in their worship of Demeter, the goddess of agriculture, and Dionysius, the giver of grapes. From these early services, the Greeks gradually developed a theater in which masks became an important feature.

The early Greek plays retold the stories of legendary characters, and masks helped to give these characters heroic grandeur and superhuman qualities. A short, spindly, ugly man who wanted to play the part of a magnificent Greek hero, like Heracles or Odysseus, could play the part well when he was properly costumed. A huge mask, which came down over his shoulders, made him look impressive and handsome. Padded robes made him look big; and buckskin shoes with thick soles made him look tall. This same man could play the part of a goddess (only men were actors) if he wore a beautiful mask.

There were other advantages in using masks. Only three actors were allowed to have speaking parts in the Greek theater, but one man could play several roles by changing masks.

The Greek plays were produced in large amphitheaters, and were often viewed by as many as 40,000 spectators. As the masks were huge, and always the same for each character, they helped the spectators identify the heroes and villains of the play.

A Greek mask was carefully constructed of painted canvas. A brass megaphone installed in the mouth amplified the actor's voice and made it carry to the vast audience.

There were two main types of Greek plays: tragedies which told of heroes who almost always died unhappily, and comedies in which characters made fun of foolish practices of the day. Each type of play had its special masks.

52

Masks of Mystery and Miracle Plays

Priests of the early Christian church wore masks in certain ceremonies and in plays which dramatized Bible stories and stories of the saints. Then, in 1207, Pope Innocent III forbade the clergy to wear masks, so people began to give plays outside the church in the churchyard. Plays based on Bible stories were called *mystery plays;* and plays based on lives of the saints were called *miracle plays.* Some actors in these plays wore disguises, and some did not; but one character always wore a mask—the devil.

There was no standard disguise for the devil. In one play, he might look something like a cat; in another, like an animal with a pointed snout; and in another, like an ugly man. He usually had horns, sometimes long and sometimes short. He always wore a costume with a tail.

On the continent of Europe, the town government produced the play; but in England, the trade guilds took charge, with each guild acting out a different scene. These English plays combined the entertainment of the theater and the fun of watching a parade. Each guild built its stage on a wagon. People gathered in different specified locations in town.

When it was time for the play to start, the first guild performed the first scene in the first location, and then moved on to the second location where the scene was repeated. The second guild then performed the second scene in the first location. In this way, the audience at each location saw all the scenes in the correct order, one after the other.

Gradually these plays became more elaborate, and more costly; yet the stage properties remained quite simple. One of the favorite settings was the mouth of Hell: huge jaws, painted red and belching smoke. A masked devil always jumped out of the jaws calling, "Ho! Ho! Ho!" At the end of the scene the devil picked up his wooden pitchfork and tossed all the lost souls into the jaws of Hell. Then he, too, popped inside.

Devil mask for mystery play. From the Hunt collection. Photo by Douglas Hunt.

Masks and Merry-Making

Masks and merry-making go hand in hand in modern European festivals. These festivals range all the way from grand costume balls given in castles to traditional festivals held in small villages.

One colorful village festival is the Dance of Phantoms, held every third year in the little village of Imst, in the mountainous region of the Austrian Tyrol. The theme of the festival is the fight between Winter and Spring for domination of Nature. Everyone hopes, of course, that Spring will overcome Winter and bring good crops during the coming summer and fall.

Only men take part in this festival. The traditional characters include: an old witch, whose ugly wooden mask has goggly eyes, fang-like teeth, and pig bristles for hair; a masked Squirter who goes among the crowd, squirting water here and there; and a masked Sack-Holder who throws grain among the spectators. There is also the lovely maiden Spring—a beauty, except for the clod-hopper boots her male impersonator is likely to wear. Everywhere bells jangle to drive evil spirits away from beautiful Spring.

In another village in the Alps, peasants clean their chimneys in the early spring. Then three days before Lent, masked men pop out of the chimneys, wearing special clothing, inside out. Women lock the doors of their homes as men run through the streets, bellowing like bulls to drive out demons and cure ills. The masked men strike passersby with switches and throw ashes on them if they can. They try to burst into homes and frighten young girls. Of course, it is all in fun; but few men would act this way if they were not masked.

Giant witch of Imst festival. Photograph courtesy of United Press International.

How to Make a Kari Hunt Mask

Would you like to make a mask like the ones used in TV shows, parades, theater plays, movies, or department store displays? You can copy the design of a mask worn by a primitive man on one of the seven continents or one of the islands of the seas. Or you can create a mask of your own. This mask won't be a quicky-false-face, like one you may have popped together for Halloween, because it takes time to make a really good mask. However, if you follow directions, you can make a mask of which you can be proud, a mask that will last as long as you care to keep it.

The easiest mask to make is one which covers only the face, and not the ears or the top of the head.

You probably have the following material and equipment on hand: black and white newspaper, colored comic sheets of newspaper, brown paper bags used to carry groceries, cord elastic, drawing board or other firm surface on which to work, wax paper or Saran Wrap, gummed tape, paint brushes, scissors, spatula or orange-wood stick or tongue depressor, three large bowls or pails to hold water.

You will need to buy the following materials in order to get the best results:

1. SOFT GRAY PLASTICINE, which you can get at a paint or art store. You will need from two to five pounds, depending on whether or not you want to make a big nose, thick lips, heavy eyebrows, etc. You can keep it for years and use it over and over again. Cover it when not in use to keep it clean.

2. PASTE. A powder, NF white, also called tapioca dextrin is the best and may be purchased at a laboratory supply house and at some drugstores. One pound is enough for twelve head masks. To mix the paste, boil a cup of water and gradually add the powder paste until you have a soupy mixture. About one half cup of powder will do. Put the paste in a glass jar with a cover and store in the refrigerator. You can also use liquid library paste.

3. A BOWL, 6 inches in diameter, and 3 inches deep. This serves as a mold.

4. STIFF COTTON BATTING, the inexpensive kind used at the base of Christmas trees, as filling for quilts, etc. This is not essential. It is used as a filler to cut down on the amount of plasticine needed. It can be used again.

5. CLEAR LACQUER AND CLEANER FOR BRUSHES.

6. TEMPERA PAINT, also called poster paint. You will need the six basic colors and might also like to have brown and gray and shades of the colors that you need for your special mask. Do not use oil paints. They make a mask look shiny, especially under artificial light.

7. FINE GRADE SANDPAPER.

MODELING THE MASK

Before you start to work, read all the directions and make sure that you have the necessary material and equipment. Ask permission to work in a certain place since your mask must remain undisturbed for several days. Cover your work space, including the work table and floor under and around it, with newspapers. Don't be any more messy than necessary.

Turn the bowl upside down on the drawing board so that you have a firm base on which to work. Cover the bowl with a layer of cotton. Cover the cotton with wax paper or Saran Wrap to keep the cotton from sticking to the plasticine.

Take a hunk of plasticine and squeeze it between your hands until it is soft and pliable. Punch it with your fingers. Make grooves with your thumbs. See how it responds to your touch. Every artist must get the feel of his material before he can begin to work.

Flatten this softened plasticine into the shape of a large thick pancake. Lay it on the mold. Cover the mold completely with flattened plasticine, making sure that it comes down over the sides and onto the drawing board. This anchors the mold and prevents its slipping as you work on details of the face.

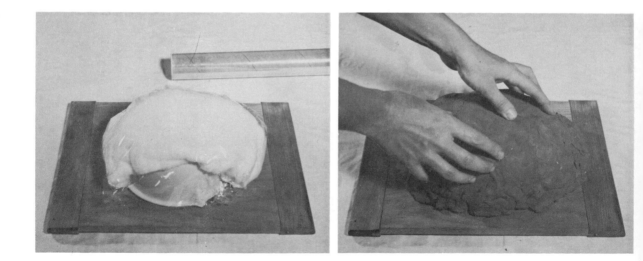

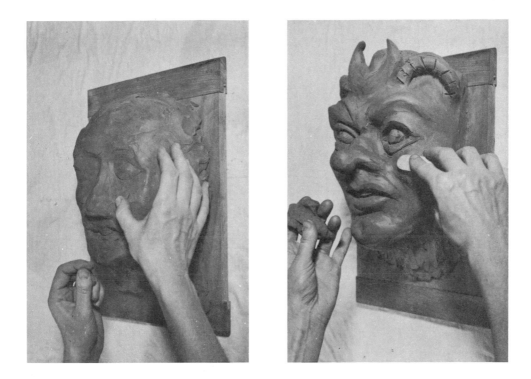

Soften more plasticine and add it to the mold until you have the general shape of a face without the nose, lips, chin, etc. A mask for a male face is usually 7½ inches from hairline to chin and a female face mask 7 inches from hairline to chin.

Using a spatula, orange stick, or wooden tongue depressor, mark the positions of the features.

Soften more plasticine between the palms of your hands and roll it into the shape of a snake. Break off a piece about 1 inch long. Working with your forefinger and your thumb, add the plasticine to the face. Gradually build up the nose, eyebrows, cheeks, and chin by piece after piece of plasticine with each piece overlapping the one next to it. Round out the cheeks. Fashion the eyes. Make lines, if you want them, with the spatula or tongue depressor. Don't be afraid to make bold features.

Don't hurry this part of the mask making. You need not complete the mold in one sitting, or even one day. When you are satisfied with your model, you are ready to make the mask.

61

PAPERING THE MASK

You are now ready to cover the plasticine mold with laminated papier mâché, that is layers of paper stuck together. You will use three kinds of paper: two double sheets of large-size black and white newspaper, two double sheets of colored comic newspaper, and two large-size brown paper bags, used to carry groceries. It is better to prepare too much paper than to suddenly find that you have too little.

Tear the double sheets of newspaper, the comic paper, and the paper bags into strips, 3 inches by 6 inches, and soak in water for a day. Do not cut the paper with scissors, because straight edges make ridges on a mask.

This mask will have three layers of paper which will make it strong enough for use or display. (Masks in the Hunt collection have only three layers and some of them are more than thirty years old.) Using three different kinds of paper will help you tell when you have finished applying one layer.

It is best to complete this part of the work in one sitting because you must not let the mask dry out while putting on the paper. If you must leave it, for even a short time, cover it with damp rags.

Lay the strips of wet comics-section paper on the plasticine mold in a horizontal position. Overlap the edges of each strip, pressing it gently with your fingers to make sure that the paper is following the curves of the plasticine and that there are no air bubbles. Bring the paper down over the edges of the mask, letting the end of the strips extend onto the drawing board.

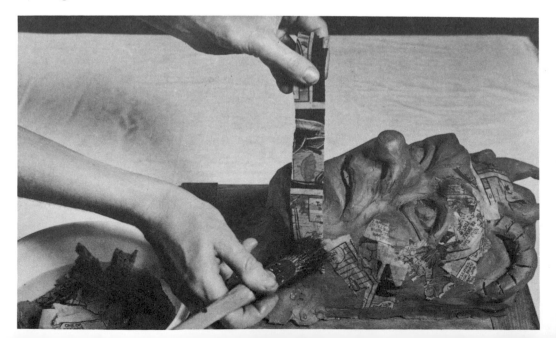

When the mold is completely covered with paper, cover the paper with paste. Rub it onto the paper gently with your fingers, as a woman rubs cold cream onto her face. Be sure to use enough paste and be sure to cover every bit of paper. Wipe off excess paste with your fingers.

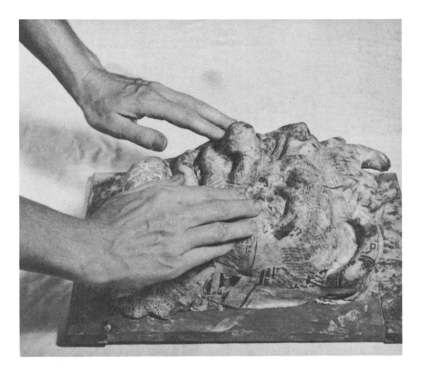

Now, cover the pasted first layer of paper with strips of wet news paper. Lay the strips in a vertical position, overlapping the edges of each strip. Tamp the paper firmly with your fingers to make sure that the layers are stuck together and to get out all the air bubbles. If you have an old shaving brush with stiff worn bristles, tamp the paper with that. Every bit of the first layer of paper must be covered with the second layer of paper.

Again cover the paper completely with paste, rubbing it gently over the entire surface. Now lay the strips of brown paper on the mold in a horizontal position (like the first layer), making sure that you overlap the edges and cover the mold completely.

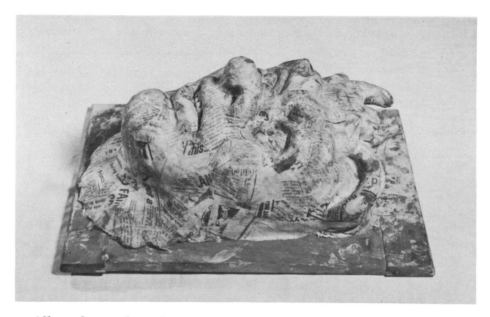

Allow the mask to dry in a warm place. It usually takes several days for it to become completely dry. If you want to hasten drying, use an electric hair dryer, but be careful not to get it too hot. You might melt the plasticine and have a mess!

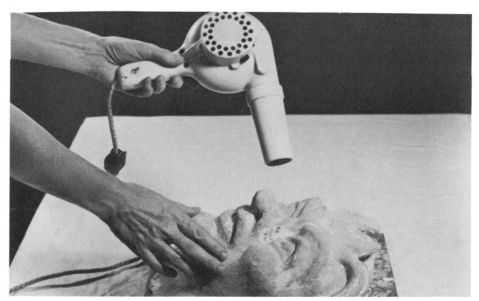

FINISHING THE MASK

When the mask is completely dry, sandpaper it gently with fine sand-paper to get a smooth surface. Remove the bowl, cotton, and wax paper. Gently pull the plasticine from the paper, making sure that you remove every bit from each crease and wrinkle. Now you have a papershell mask, and you have destroyed the mold, so there will never be another mask exactly like the one you have made.

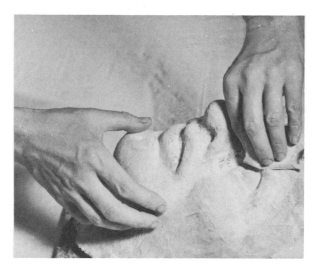

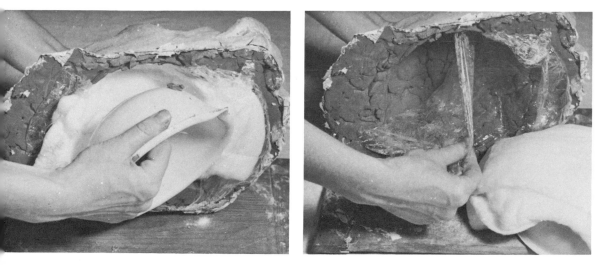

Cut away straggling ends of paper at the edge of the mask. Wet wide gummed tape and put it on the edge of the mask to make a binder, with half of the tape on the outside and half on the inside. (If you do not have gummed tape, cut a strip of paper 1½ inches wide and paste this on the edge as a binder.)

Hold the mask up to the light to see if there are any weak spots. If there are, patch them on the outside of the mask with bits of pasted paper. Let the paper dry. Sandpaper the mask again gently.

Paint the mask with a fine layer of clear lacquer to set the paper.

When the lacquer is dry, paint the mask, using tempera colors (poster paints). They give the dull colors you want; and if you make a slight mistake, you can wipe off the paint with a wet cloth. The masks need two coats of paint.

For the first layer of paint, mix white, brown, and red to make a complexion tone. Don't be disappointed when you see it on the mask. The purpose of the first layer is to cover the paper and to make a background for the other painting.

Hold the mask to your face and make sure that the eyes are where you want them. Mark the spots for holes. Pupils should be 2½ inches apart. Do not cut them out until the mask has been painted a second time.

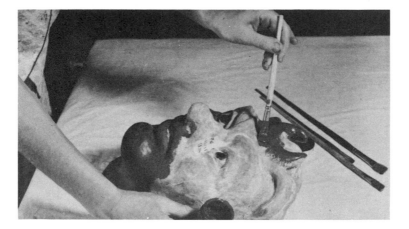

Painting the second coat is fun, because your mask comes alive and takes on character. You can paint entirely with a brush. Or you can use your fingers to apply color to get the tones you want on the large areas, such as cheeks, forehead, and chin; and use a brush to paint details.

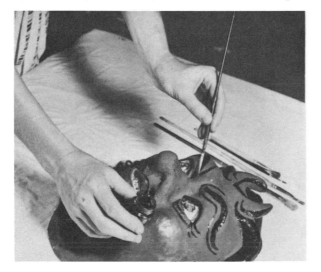

When the paint is dry, cut out the pupils of the eyes and paint the *inside* edge of the pupils black, to make them stand out. Paint the inside of the mask a buff or white color to preserve it and make it more desirable to wear.

To attach an elastic for holding the mask in place on the face, punch small holes at points on the gummed tape, ½ inch from the edges of the mask, and in line with the outside corners of the eyes. Cut elastic the correct length and tie in place.

When your mask is finished, put it on.
Do you feel transformed or are you merely disguised?

Source Materials

BOOKS

Carrighar, Sally. *Moonlight at Midday* (Knopf, 1959)

Coast, John. *Dancers of Bali* (Putnam 1953)

Covarrubias, Miguel. *Island of Bali* (Knopf, 1937)

Dorian, Edith M., and Wilson, W. N. *Hokahey! American Indians Then and Now* (Whittlesley, 1957)

Dumartre, Pierre Louis. *The Italian Comedy* (G. G. Harrop, London, 1929)

Gregor, Josef. *Masks of the World* (B. T. Batsford, London, 1937)

Griaule, Marcel. *Art de l'Afrique Noire* (Les Editions du Chene, Paris, 1947)

Hofsinde, Robert. *Indian's Secret World* (Wm. Morrow, 1955)

Kjersmeier, Carl. *African Negro Sculptures* (A. Zwemmer, London, 1948)

Mantzius, Karl. *History of Theatrical Art In Ancient and Modern Times* (Peter Smith, 1937)

Nicoll, Allardyce. *Development of the Theatre* (Harcourt, Brace, 1937)

Nicoll, Allardyce. *Masks, Mimes, and Miracles* (Harcourt, Brace, 1931)

Powell, Doane. *Masks and How to Make Them* (Bridgeman, 1948)

Riley, Olive Lasette. *Masks and Magic* (Studio Books, 1955)

Stopes, Marie C. and Sakurai, Joji. *Plays of Old Japan, The Nō* (Dutton, 1913)

Thomas, Lowell, Jr. *Out of This World* (Garden City, 1954)

PAMPHLETS

American Museum of Natural History, New York City. *Masks,* Wissler, Karl. Science Guide No. 96, 1946

Brooklyn Museum, Institute of Arts and Science, Brooklyn, N.Y. *Masks, Barabaric and Civilized,* Spinden, Herbert, 1939

Cranbrook Institute of Science, Bloomfield Hills, Mich.
  An Exhibition of Masks, Ocult and Utilitarian, 1940
  The Iroquois, Speck, Frank G., 1945

Denver Art Museum, Denver, Colo.
  Types of Indian Masks, leaflet 65-66, 1935

Field Museum of Natural History, Chicago, Ill.
  Oriental Theatricals, Laufer, Berthold, Guide, part 1, 1923

Newark Museum, Newark, N.J.
  Skulls and Bones, 1912
  Tibetan Collection, Edward N. Crane Memorial

Royal Ontario Museum of Toronto, Toronto, Canada
  Masks, The Many Faces of Man, 1959

University Museum, University of Pennsylvania, Philadelphia, Pa.
  Masks, Vol. 13, No. 1, 1947
  Masking in Eastern North America, Speck, Frank G., Vol. 15, No. 1, 1950

MAGAZINES

Asia, June '41, "Masks"
Coronet, Feb. '49, "There's Magic in Masks"
Harpers Weekly, April 9, '10, "Masks from the Forbidden Land," Beasley, Walter L.
International Studio, Nov. '23, "Masks and Their Meaning," Mac-Gowan, Kenneth
National Geographic, (The)
  Aug. '36, "Merry Makers of Imst"
  Nov. '59, "Tukuna Maidens Come of Age," Schultz, Harold
National History
  July-Aug. '28, "Lore of the Demon Masks," Wissler, Clark
  June '46, "Masks and Men," Mead, Margaret
New York Times Magazine
  April 15, '51, "Magic of the Mask," Shapiro, H. L.
  May 31, '59, "Science Psychiatry or Witchery," Huxley, Elspeth

Science News Letter
    July 20, '46, "A World of Masks," Morrow, Martha G.
Scientific American
    Aug. 16, '02, "Group of Indian Masks," Yeigh, Frank
    Oct. 6 & 13, '06, "Masks of Classic and Modern Times," Geare, Randolph I.
Time Magazine
    May 20, '46, "False Faces"
    June 9, '52, "Death and the Devil"